CH 4-95

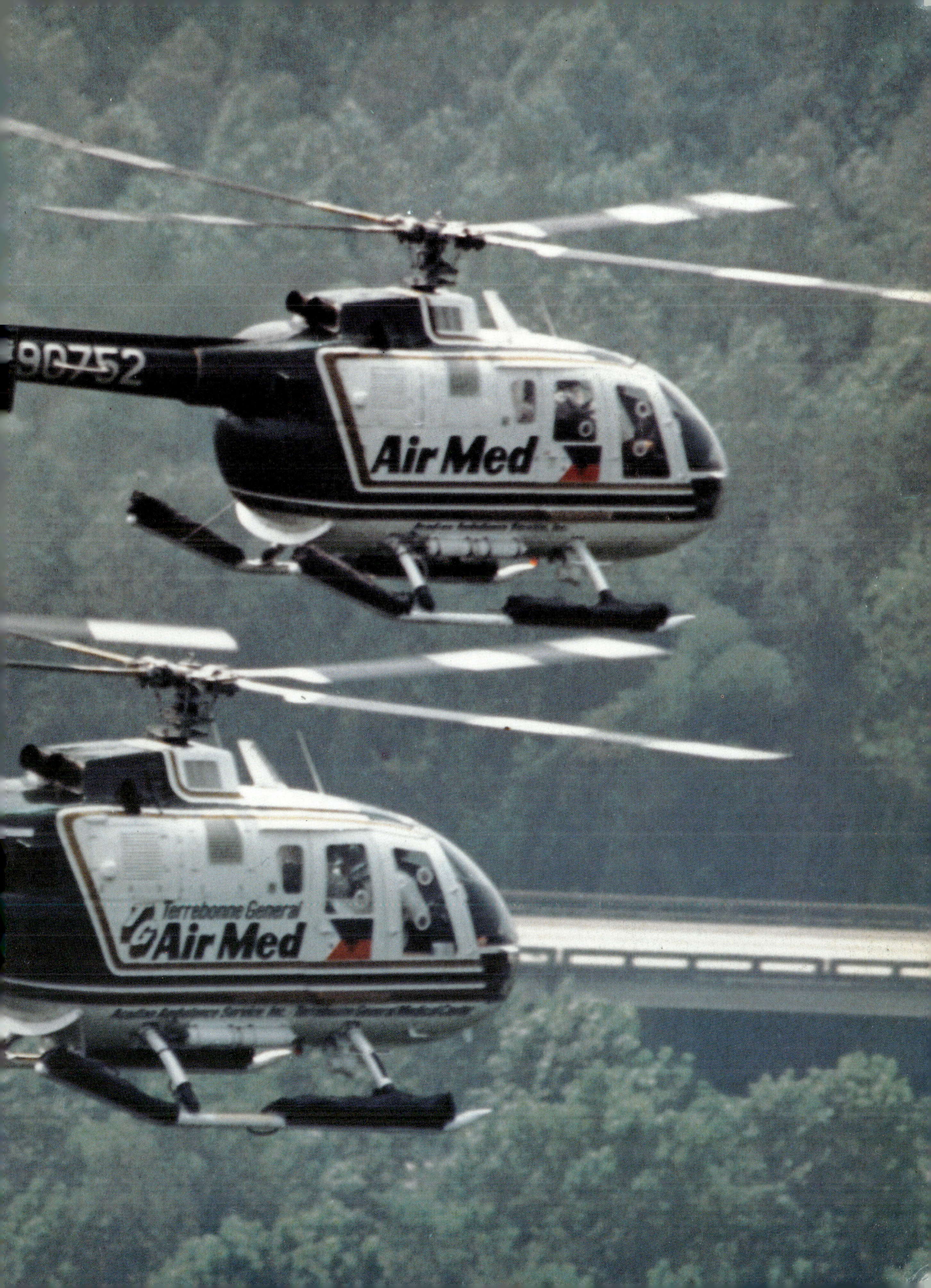
90752
Air Med
Terrebonne General
Air Med

© 1990 Franklin Watts

Franklin Watts Inc
387 Park Avenue South
New York NY 10016

Library of Congress Cataloging-in-Publication Data
Barrett, Norman S.
    The picture world of air rescue / Norman Barrett.
       p. cm. — (Picture world)
    Summary: A look at the types of aircraft used to rescue people from remote, often inaccessible places
    ISBN 0–531–14089–X
    1. Search and rescue operations—Juvenile literature.   [1. Rescue work.] I. Title. II. Series.
    TL553.8.B37   1991
    629.133'3—dc20   90–31222
                                                            CIP AC

Printed in Belgium
All rights reserved

Designed by
K and Co

Photographs by
RAF High Wycombe
U.S. Department of Defense
MBB
Australia House
Bell Helicopter Textron
Westland Helicopters
U.S. Coast Guard
Steve Strike
British Forces Hong Kong
Paul Berriff Productions in
   association with Scottish TV

Technical Consultant
RAF High Wycombe

The Picture World of
Air Rescue

Norman Barrett

CONTENTS

Introduction	6
Helicopter rescue	8
Military rescue	17
Air ambulances	18
Rescue and reconnaissance planes	22
Flying doctors	24
Facts	26
Glossary	28
Index	29

Franklin Watts
New York • London • Sydney • Toronto

Introduction

Planes and helicopters are used to search for and rescue people in difficulties at sea or on land. Planes are fast and can search wide areas, while helicopters can land in difficult places or save people by hoisting them up into the cabin.

Aircraft may also be used to carry emergency supplies to places hit by disasters such as floods. Some are also equipped for emergency medical duties, functioning as flying ambulances.

▽ A flying ambulance operated by a medical center. Helicopters are now used in many parts of the world for regular ambulance work.

▷ Even when a helicopter cannot land, people can be hoisted up as it hovers in the air.

▽ Feed is dropped from a plane for cattle stranded by flooding.

Helicopter rescue

Rescue helicopters often have a crew of three or four — a pilot and perhaps a copilot, a hoistman, and a radar operator.

The craft is flown by the pilot and navigated by either the copilot or the radar operator, who also operates the hoist.

The key crew member is the hoistman, who is lowered on a line in order to bring up injured or stranded victims.

▷ A mountain rescue team carries a victim up a hillside in a special stretcher that can be hoisted into the hovering helicopter.

▽ The hoistman grasps a victim's wrist as he prepares to fasten him in a harness. The hoist operator, in the cabin door, is ready to reel them in.

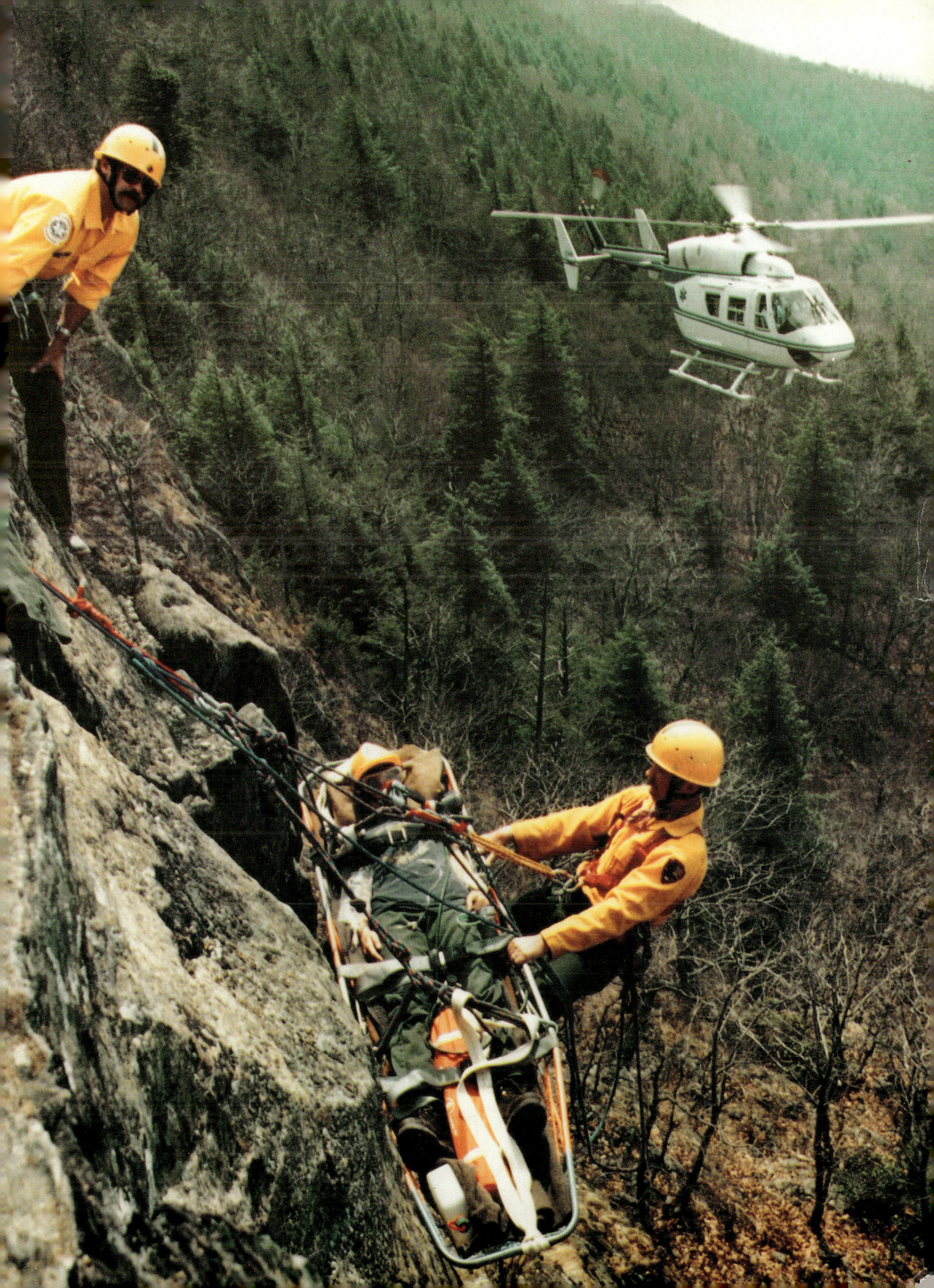

For mountain rescues, the hoistman wears special survival clothing and climbing boots. He carries a backpack with food and a sleeping bag, in case he is stranded.

At sea, the hoistman wears an all-in-one immersion suit and a lifejacket.

Hoistmen are highly trained in first aid. They are responsible for all the medical supplies and rescue equipment on the helicopter.

△ A helicopter crew practicing a double lift. This is a quick method used for rescuing an uninjured survivor. The hoistman hooks the survivor to the hoist, places a strap around his body and uses his legs to steady the survivor as they are reeled in.

▷ A victim is carried into a helicopter that has landed on a snowy slope. Helicopters are ideal emergency vehicles for skiing accidents or for rescuing people stranded in the snow.

▽ A helicopter that has crashed. Rescue helicopters often have to fly in terrible conditions. This crash was caused by a "whiteout" — the falling snow made it impossible for the pilot to see.

At sea, helicopters often find it dangerous to hover directly above boats such as fishing vessels because of the chances of the hoist line getting tangled with radio masts or rigging. In such cases a technique called a hi-line transfer may be used.

With this method, a line from the hoist hook is dropped to the deck and controlled by a member of the ship's crew.

△ The hoistman swings down for a sea rescue, waiting for the crew of the boat below to pull him toward the deck with a line attached to the hoist hook.

▷ A close-up of the hoistman as he dangles above the waves.

▽ The first survivors are hoisted up to safety from the sinking fishing vessel.

Special teams are trained for mountain rescue. They might have to go to the aid of injured climbers or people trapped by an avalanche. They may be lifted by helicopter as close to the scene of the accident as possible.

Dog teams may also be needed for mountain rescue. They are used to help find victims, especially at night or if people are buried in an avalanche.

▽ A mountain rescue team with specially trained dogs wait to enter a rescue helicopter.

△ Fire departments in some cities use helicopters for rescue operations. They can reach people trapped on the tops of tall buildings.

▷ An air force helicopter on flood relief duty. Armed forces are often brought in to deliver food and medical supplies during civil emergencies.

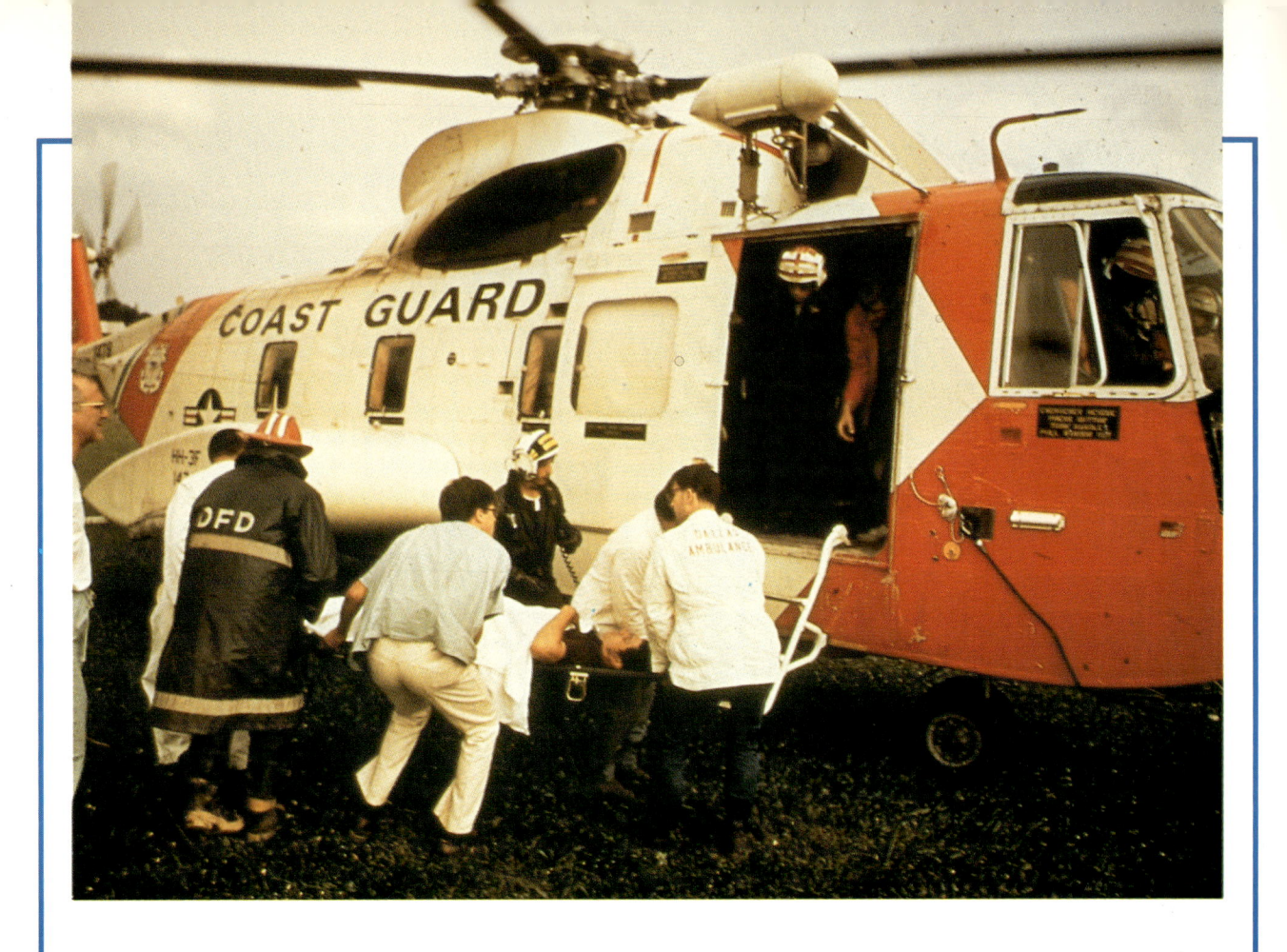

△ A victim being transferred from a U.S. Coast Guard helicopter to a hospital. In the United States the Coast Guard is a branch of the armed services. But it also serves as protector of life and property at sea.

◁ A helicopter helps to guide sheep to higher ground away from flooded areas.

Military rescue

Helicopters are used in wartime to evacuate injured troops from the battlefield. They may also be used to rescue troops trapped behind enemy lines.

Military helicopters may be equipped to serve as field hospitals. Trained medical staff provide emergency treatment on the way to the hospital. The largest helicopters can carry 20 or more casualties.

▽ Wounded troops are carried into a rescue helicopter during the Vietnam War.

Air ambulances

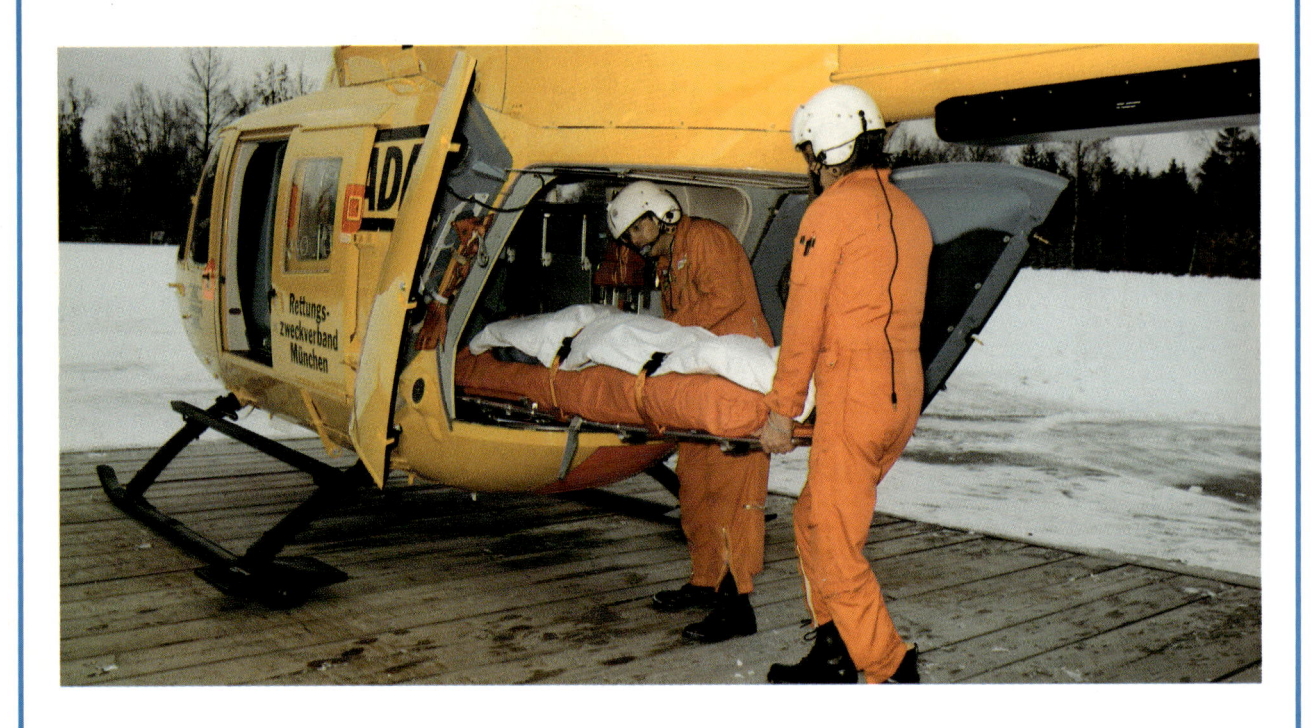

Helicopters and planes are part of the ambulance service in some countries. They are crewed by "paramedics," people trained to give first aid and drugs, and use lifesaving apparatus.

In cities, helicopters provide a fast, direct service, avoiding the traffic. They can also cover areas of forests, mountains, or water that road vehicles cannot reach. Planes are sometimes used for transporting patients over long distances.

△ A victim is stretchered in through the wide back doors of a helicopter ambulance. These flying ambulances are equipped to treat patients and keep serious casualties alive while enroute to the hospital.

△ People watch a demonstration by paramedics, carrying a "victim" to a waiting flying ambulance. Helicopters can land in a city's open spaces or speed to highway accidents without getting caught in traffic.

▷ The inside of a flying ambulance, equipped with all kinds of lifesaving apparatus and even an incubator (center) for a newborn baby.

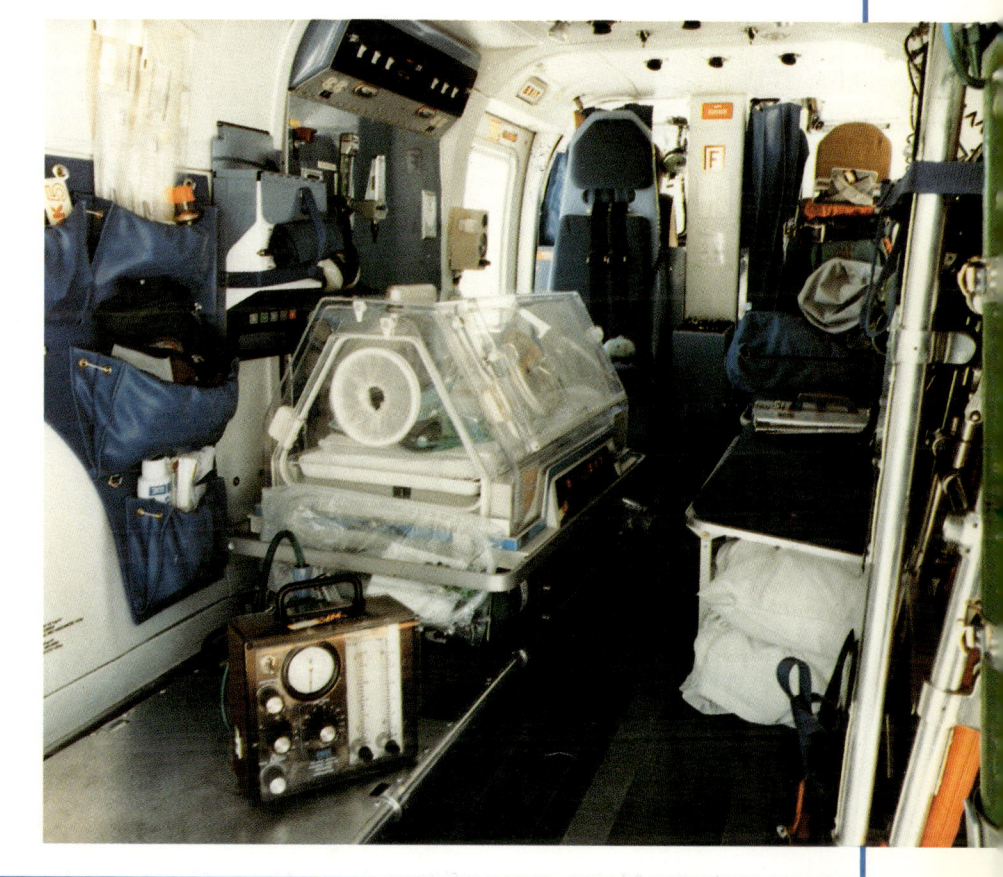

△ A victim is stretchered out of a flying ambulance onto a hospital trolley. Some hospitals have marked areas, or helipads, for the helicopters to land on.

△ A converted DC-9 airliner, this C-9A Nightingale is part of a fleet of "flying hospitals" used by the U.S. Air Force. They transport civil as well as military patients from bases around the world.

▷ Inside, the Nightingale is equipped to carry 40 litter (bed) patients as well as 40 in seats.

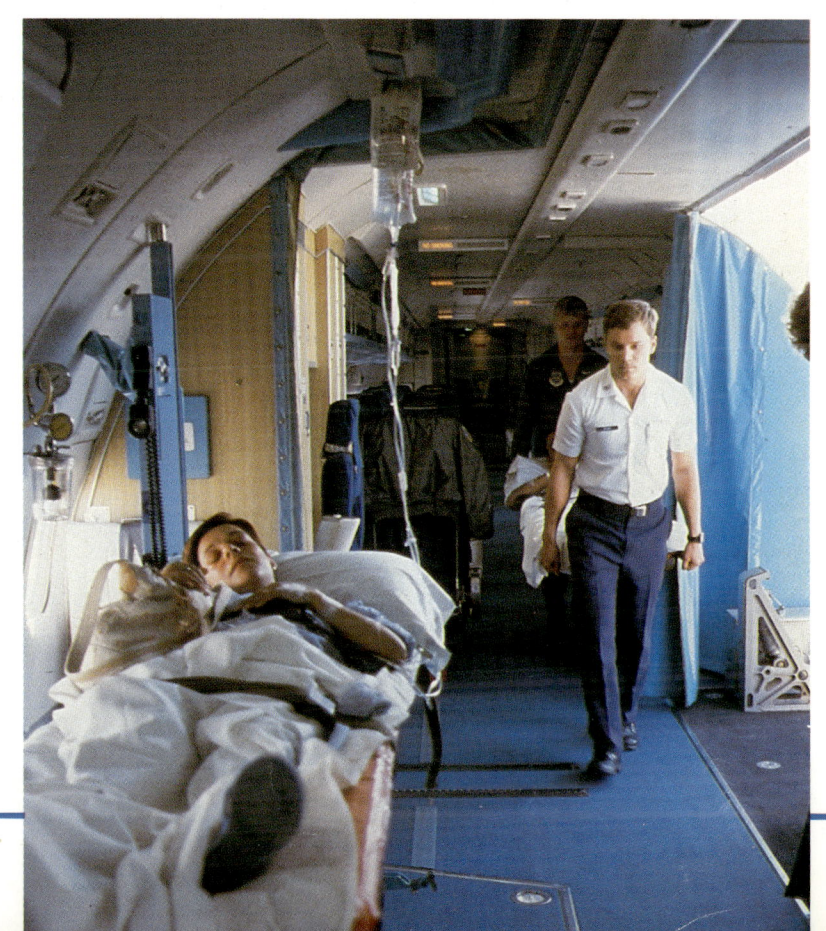

21

Rescue and reconnaissance planes

In some parts of the world airplanes are used in search and rescue work. They can cover large distances quickly, and search wide areas. They radio information back to base.

Planes drop provisions to communities cut off by floods or other disasters. They provide emergency supplies that might take days or even weeks to arrive by road.

▽ "You hail we bale" is the slogan painted on a rescue plane in Australia. Planes are used for dropping emergency supplies and livestock feed over areas affected by floods.

Reconnaissance aircraft are used in civil search and rescue work, especially over remote areas. Their highly sensitive equipment can detect craft at night over great distances and in all kinds of weather.

Many reconnaissance planes carry survival kits. They drop these by parachute to the victims, and radio their location to rescue helicopters or to lifeboats or other ships for a sea rescue.

△ A Nimrod, a reconnaissance plane of the Royal Air Force. Specially equipped military aircraft such as these often help in civil search and rescue operations.

Flying doctors

The Royal Flying Doctor service of Australia provides emergency medical treatment for people in remote parts of the continent.

Many people live and work in places hundreds of miles from the nearest doctor. With 14 radio bases covering the whole continent, "flying doctors" are sent out to treat accident victims on the spot or to attend to people too sick to be moved.

△ A Flying Doctor aircraft over Alice Springs, in Australia's central desert. In much of Australia's interior, or "outback," settlements are separated by vast distances.

△ Flying doctors in the plane's cabin, on their way to tend patients in the "outback." Some communities have their own small hospitals, but no resident doctors.

▷ A patient is brought back to base by plane for treatment in a hospital.

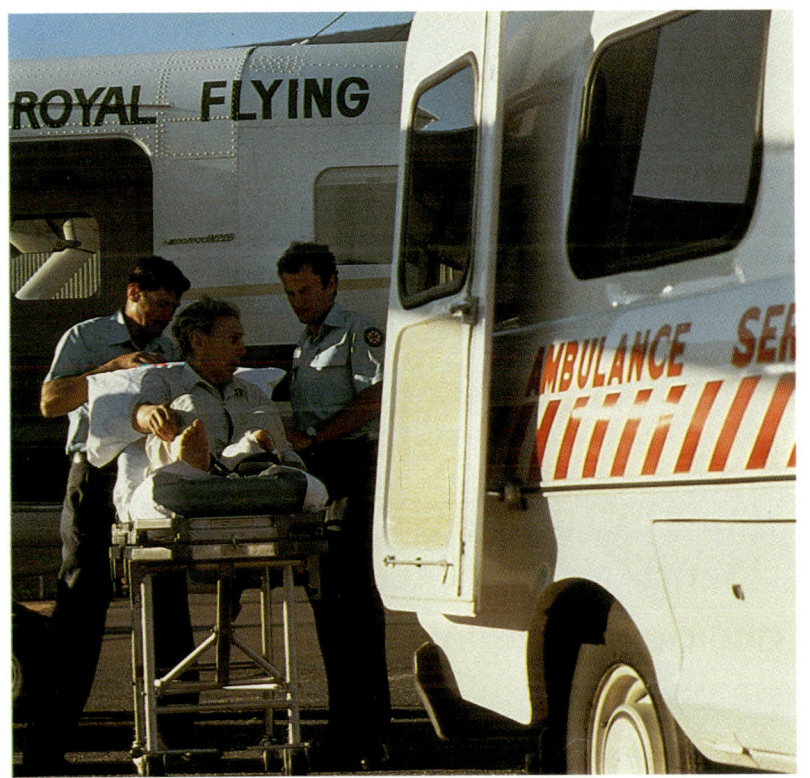

25

Facts

Hooking on the line
Military lifejackets have special loops on them. These are for a helicopter hoist attachment called a "Grabbit" hook, which can be used to hoist them out of the water. Grabbit hooks are also used for securing harnesses and stretchers.

△ The Grabbit hook on the end of a hoist line.

Berlin airlift
One of the biggest air rescues of all time was the Berlin airlift of 1948. For 15 months, American, British, and French airmen flew vital supplies into West Berlin, which had been blockaded by Russian troops. During this time, 277,000 flights carried in over 2 million tons of food and other supplies.

First helicopter rescue
The first recorded combat helicopter rescue operation took place in Burma in 1944. A tiny Sikorsky YR-4, whose crew was just the pilot, Lieutenant Carter Harman of the U.S. Air Commandos, made two missions into Japanese-held territory to rescue four men. Three were injured or sick British soldiers, the fourth their American pilot whose plane had failed. The helicopter had to carry an extra fuel tank strapped to its roof to give it the necessary range.

Giant to the rescue
One of the world's largest rescue helicopters is the Sikorsky HH-53C of the U.S. Air Force. It is known as the Super Jolly Green Giant. It can

△ The Super Jolly Green Giant, one of the largest rescue helicopters.

lift more than 20 survivors and has a range of about 1,000 km (600 miles) without refueling. It is also one of the few helicopters that can be refueled in the air.

Super Jolly Green Giants have highly specialized crews, including "para-rescue-jumpers," who are trained as parachutists, subaqua divers, marksmen, and survival experts. The helicopters are sometimes called out to help in civil rescue operations.

Saigon airlift
The biggest civil rescue mission undertaken by helicopters took place in Saigon before American troops left in 1973. A total of 7,400 people were airlifted out of Saigon in 590 missions to waiting U.S. Navy ships. Fifty Vietnamese helicopters had to be ditched because of shortage of space on the ships.

Landing on water
The Sea King helicopter can land on water. It is fitted on each side with floats called "sponsons." The regular landing gear is drawn up inside these when necessary.

△ The wheels of the Sea King may be retracted into the sponsons for landing on water.

27

Glossary

Avalanche
A great fall of snow, ice, and rock down a mountainside, sometimes burying people in its path.

Flying ambulance
An aircraft equipped as an ambulance and used for regular ambulance work.

Grabbit hook
A hook on the end of a hoist line.

Helipad
A special area for helicopters to land on.

Hi-line transfer
A method often used for lowering the hoistman onto small boats, when there is a danger of getting caught up in the rigging. A line is dropped to the boat and controlled by a member of its crew.

Hoist
Equipment for lowering or raising people or things from a rescue helicopter.

Hoistman
The member of the helicopter crew who is lowered and raised on a line.

Paramedics
Crew trained to treat casualties or sick people on the spot and on the way to the hospital. They are usually qualified to give drugs and injections and to use specialized lifesaving apparatus.

Reconnaissance
Scouring the sea or land to look for survivors or gather information.

Sponsons
Special floats that enable some helicopters to land on water.

Whiteout
When a pilot cannot see because of falling snow, it is called a whiteout.

Index

accident 14, 19
air ambulance 18
air force 15, 23
airliner 21
ambulance 18
avalanche 14, 28

backpack 10
Berlin airlift 26
buildings 15

cattle 7
climbing boots 10
coast guard 16
copilot 8
crash 11

disaster 6, 22
doctor 24, 25
dog 14
double lift 10

field hospital 17
fire department 15
fishing vessel 12, 13
flood, flooding 6, 7, 15, 16, 22
flying ambulance 6, 18, 19, 20, 28
flying doctor 24, 25
flying hospital 21

Grabbit hook 26, 28

harness 8, 26
helicopter 6, 7, 8, 9, 10, 11, 12, 14, 15, 16, 17, 18, 20, 23, 26, 27
helipad 20, 28
hi-line transfer 12, 28

hoist, hoisting 6, 7, 8, 12, 26, 28
hoist hook 12, 26
hoistman 8, 10, 12, 13, 28
hoist operator 8
hospital 16, 17, 18, 20, 25

immersion suit 10
incubator 19

lifeboat 23
lifejacket 10, 26
litter 21

mountain rescue 9, 10, 14

parachute 23
paramedic 18, 19, 28
pilot 8, 11
plane, airplane 6, 7, 18, 21, 22, 23, 24, 25

radar operator 8
radio 22, 23, 24
reconnaissance 23, 28

Saigon airlift 27
sleeping bag 10
snow 11
sponson 27, 28
stretcher 9, 20, 26
Super Jolly Green Giant 26, 27
survival clothing 10
survival kit 23

Vietnam War 17

wartime 17
whiteout 11, 28

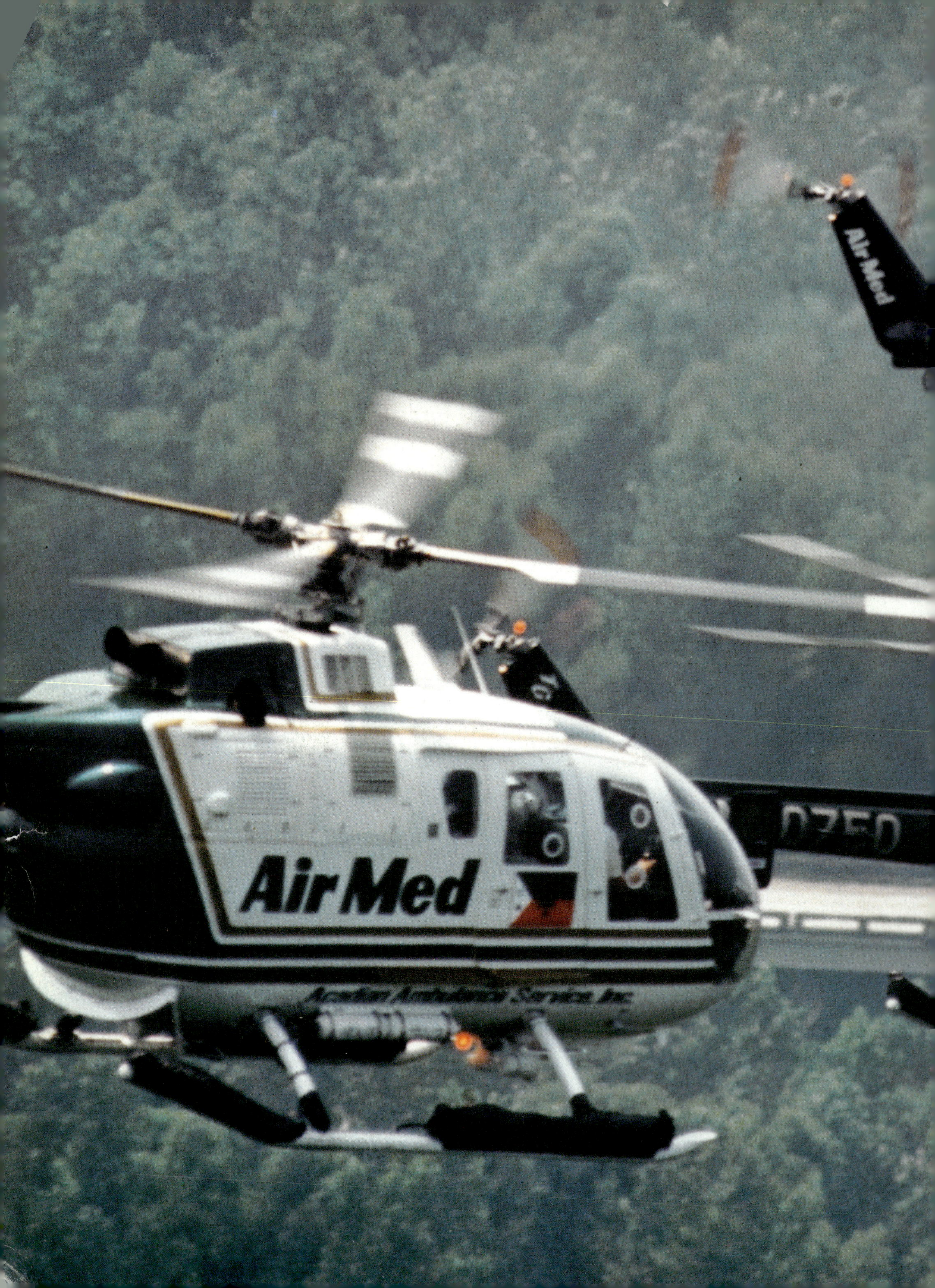
Air Med
Air Med
Acadian Ambulance Service, Inc.